THE EVOLUTION
OF AFRICA'S MAJOR NATIONS

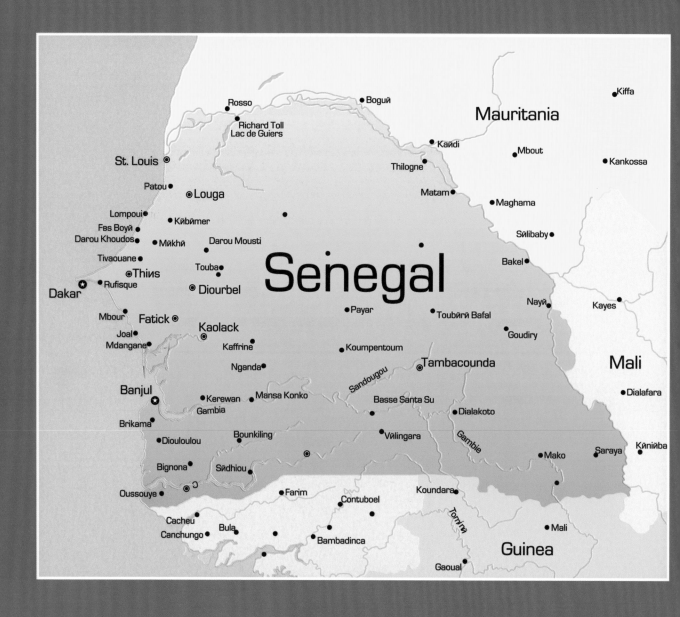

THE EVOLUTION
OF AFRICA'S MAJOR NATIONS

Senegal

Tanya Mulroy

Mason Crest
Philadelphia

Mason Crest
370 Reed Road
Broomall, PA 19008
www.masoncrest.com

Copyright © 2013 by Mason Crest, an imprint of National Highlights, Inc. All rights reserved.
Printed and bound in the Hashemite Kingdom of Jordan.

CPSIA Compliance Information: Batch #EAMN2013-20. For further information,
contact Mason Crest at 1-866-MCP-Book.

First printing

1 3 5 7 9 8 6 4 2

Library of Congress Cataloging-in-Publication Data

  Mulroy, Tanya.
   Senegal / Tanya Mulroy.
     p. cm. — (Evolution of Africa's major nations.)
   Includes bibliographical references and index.
   ISBN 978-1-4222-2201-0 (hardcover)
   ISBN 978-1-4222-2229-4 (pbk.)
   ISBN 978-1-4222-9441-3 (ebook)
   1. Senegal--Juvenile literature. I. Title. II. Series: Evolution of Africa's major nations.
   DT549.22.M85 2012
   966.3--dc22

                2011018507

Africa: Facts and Figures	Egypt	Nigeria
The African Union	Ethiopia	Rwanda
Algeria	Ghana	Senegal
Angola	Ivory Coast	Sierra Leone
Botswana	Kenya	South Africa
Burundi	Liberia	Sudan
Cameroon	Libya	Tanzania
Democratic Republic	Morocco	Uganda
of the Congo	Mozambique	Zimbabwe

Table of Contents

Introduction   6
Robert I. Rotberg

Africa's Westernmost Land   11

An Ancient Past, A Promising Future   21

Democracy in Decline?   33

A Stable Economy   39

The People of Senegal   49

Blending Past and Present   61

A Calendar of Senegalese Festivals   66

Recipes   68

Glossary   70

Project and Report Ideas   72

Chronology   74

Further Reading/Internet Resources   76

For More Information   77

Index   78

Africa: Progress, Problems, and Promise

Robert I. Rotberg

Africa is the cradle of humankind, but for millennia it was off the familiar, beaten path of global commerce and discovery. Its many peoples therefore developed largely apart from the diffusion of modern knowledge and the spread of technological innovation until the 17th through 19th centuries. With the coming to Africa of the book, the wheel, the hoe, and the modern rifle and cannon, foreigners also brought the vastly destructive transatlantic slave trade, oppression, discrimination, and onerous colonial rule. Emerging from that crucible of European rule, Africans created nationalistic movements and then claimed their numerous national independences in the 1960s. The result is the world's largest continental assembly of new countries.

There are 53 members of the African Union, a regional political grouping, and 48 of those nations lie south of the Sahara. Fifteen of them, including mighty Ethiopia, are landlocked, making international trade and economic growth that much more arduous and expensive. Access to navigable rivers is limited, natural harbors are few, soils are poor and thin, several countries largely consist of miles and miles of sand, and tropical diseases have sapped the strength and productivity of innumerable millions. Being landlocked, having few resources (although countries along Africa's west coast have tapped into deep offshore petroleum and gas reservoirs), and being beset by malaria, tuberculosis, schistosomiasis, AIDS, and many other maladies has kept much of Africa poor for centuries.

Thirty-two of the world's poorest 44 countries are African. Hunger is common. So is rapid deforestation and desertification. Unemployment rates are often over 50 percent, for jobs are few—even in agriculture. Where Africa once

Senegalese fishermen draw in their nets on an Atlantic beach..

was a land of small villages and a few large cities, with almost everyone engaged in growing grain or root crops or grazing cattle, camels, sheep, and goats, today more than half of all the more than 1 billion Africans, especially those who live south of the Sahara, reside in towns and cities. Traditional agriculture hardly pays, and a number of countries in Africa—particularly the smaller and more fragile ones—can no longer feed themselves.

There is not one Africa, for the continent is full of contradictions and variety. Of the 750 million people living south of the Sahara, at least 150 million live in Nigeria, 85 million in Ethiopia, 68 million in the Democratic Republic of the Congo, and 49 million in South Africa. By contrast, tiny Djibouti and Equatorial Guinea have fewer than 1 million people each, and prosperous

Villagers greet personnel distributing humanitarian assistance. Most of Senegal's very poor live in the rural parts of the country.

Botswana and Namibia each are under 2.2 million in population. Within some countries, even medium-sized ones like Zambia (12 million), there are a plethora of distinct ethnic groups speaking separate languages. Zambia, typical with its multitude of competing entities, has 70 such peoples, roughly broken down into four language and cultural zones. Three of those languages jostle with English for primacy.

Given the kaleidoscopic quality of African culture and deep-grained poverty, it is no wonder that Africa has developed economically and politically less rapidly than other regions. Since independence from colonial rule, weak governance has also plagued Africa and contributed significantly to the widespread poverty of its peoples. Only Botswana and offshore Mauritius have been governed democratically without interruption since independence. Both are among Africa's wealthiest countries, too, thanks to the steady application of good governance.

Aside from those two nations, and South Africa, Africa has been a continent of coups since 1960, with massive and oil-rich Nigeria suffering incessant periods of harsh, corrupt, autocratic military rule. Nearly every other country on or around the continent, small and large, has been plagued by similar bouts of instability and dictatorial rule. In the 1970s and 1980s Idi Amin ruled Uganda capriciously and Jean-Bedel Bokassa proclaimed himself emperor of the Central African Republic. Macias Nguema of Equatorial Guinea was another in that same mold. More recently Daniel arap Moi held Kenya in thrall and Robert Mugabe has imposed himself on once-prosperous Zimbabwe. In both of those cases, as in the case of Gnassingbe Eyadema in Togo and the late Mobutu Sese Seko in Congo, these presidents stole wildly and drove entire peoples and their nations into penury. Corruption is common in Africa, and so are a weak rule-of-law framework, misplaced development, high expenditures on soldiers and low expenditures on health and education, and a widespread (but not universal) refusal on the part of leaders to work well for their followers and citizens.

Conflict between groups within countries has also been common in Africa. More than 12 million Africans have been killed in civil wars since 1990, while another 9 million have become refugees. Decades of conflict in Sudan led to a January 2011 referendum in which the people of southern Sudan voted overwhelmingly to secede and form a new state. In early 2011, anti-government protests spread throughout North Africa, ultimately toppling long-standing regimes in Tunisia and Egypt. That same year, there were serious ongoing hostilities within Chad, Ivory Coast, Libya, the Niger Delta region of Nigeria, and Somalia.

Despite such dangers, despotism, and decay, Africa is improving. Botswana and Mauritius, now joined by South Africa, Senegal, Kenya, and Ghana, are beacons of democratic growth and enlightened rule. Uganda and Senegal are taking the lead in combating and reducing the spread of AIDS, and others are following. There are serious signs of the kinds of progressive economic policy changes that might lead to prosperity for more of Africa's peoples. The trajectory in Africa is positive.

(Opposite) Traditional fishermen of the Atlantic coastal village of Toubab Dialaw prepare their canoes before setting out in search of the day's catch. (Right) A group of pelicans in the Djoudj National Park. Senegal is home to a great variety of birds and animals.

Africa's Westernmost Land

THE REPUBLIC OF SENEGAL is land of stunning coastlines, semi-desert sands, fertile river valleys, grassland plains, and moist tropical *rainforests*. The extreme variety in environments within the country sustains a rich diversity of vegetation and wildlife.

THE LAND

Located on the westernmost edge of the African continent, Senegal is slightly smaller than the state of South Dakota, covering an area of approximately 75,950 square miles (196,772 square kilometers). The country borders Guinea and Guinea-Bissau on the south, Mali on the east, and Mauritania on the north and east. Senegal also completely surrounds the narrow strip of land that comprises The Gambia. This tiny nation divides Senegal into a larg-er, northern portion and a southern region, known as *Casamance*.

Along the western border of Senegal runs a 330-mile (531-km) coast-line, which is bordered by the Atlantic Ocean. Sandy beaches predomi-nate along much of shoreline, although some areas consist of mangrove swamps and winding *estuaries*.

Most of Senegal consists of low, rolling plains that eventually rise to foothills in the southeast. The plains rarely rise higher than 200 feet (61 meters) above sea level. The country's lowest elevation is sea level, along the coast of the Atlantic. Senegal's highest point, standing at 1,906 feet (581 m), is an unnamed point near Népen Diakha, which is located in the southeastern part of the country.

Within Senegal, four major rivers flow westward toward the Atlantic Ocean. One of these waterways—the Senegal River—runs through the northern part of the country, forming the border with Mauritania. Altogether, the Senegal River stretches for a total of 1,020 miles (1,642 km), creating an extensive river basin that covers 174,000 square miles (450,000 sq km), or nearly 37 percent of Senegal's total land area. The river basin also spreads across Mauritania, Mali, and Guinea, providing water to a large portion of the West African region. The river's main tributaries are the Bafing, Bakoye, and Faleme Rivers, all of which have their sources in the Fouta Djallon Mountains in Guinea.

Senegal's three other major rivers are the Saloum, Casamance, and Gambia. The wide and meandering Saloum River winds through central Senegal, while the Casamance River cuts through the south-

THE GEOGRAPHY OF SENEGAL

Location: West Africa, bordering the North Atlantic Ocean, between Guinea-Bissau and Mauritania

Area: (Slightly smaller than South Dakota)
total: 75,950 square miles (196,772 sq km)
land: 74,366 square miles (192,530 sq km)
water: 1,619 square miles (4,192 sq km)

Borders: The Gambia, 460 miles (740 km); Guinea, 205 miles (330 km); Guinea-Bissau, 210 miles (338 km); Mali, 260 miles (419 km); Mauritania, 505 miles (813 km); coastline, 330 miles (531 km)

Climate: tropical; hot, humid; rainy season (May to November) has strong southeast winds; dry season (December to April) dominated by hot, dry, *harmattan* wind

Terrain: generally low, rolling plains rising to foothills in southeast

Elevation extremes:
lowest point: Atlantic Ocean, 0 feet (0 m)
highest point: unnamed feature near Népen Diakha, 1,906 feet (581 m)

Natural hazards: lowlands seasonally flooded; periodic droughts

Source: CIA World Factbook, 2011.

western region of the country. The Gambia River flows through southeastern Senegal and through The Gambia, before emptying into the Atlantic Ocean.

CLIMATE

Senegal has a tropical climate. The weather is generally hot and humid during the rainy season, which runs from May to November, with rainfall amounts varying from year to year. The dry season generally occurs from December to April. Long periods of drought are common.

The northern part of Senegal is in the *Sahel*—a wide band of semi-arid land that lies in northern Africa, just south of the Sahara Desert. The Sahel is a transitional area where dry desert lands of North Africa eventually change over to grasslands in the south. When there is rain, the Sahel supports lush grasslands, but it reverts to more desert-like conditions in the dry season.

During that time, from December to April, the Sahel is also affected by a strong, damaging wind that ruins crops and dries out water sources. Called the *harmattan*, this sand-laden wind blows from the Sahara Desert to the west, sometimes for days at a time.

When the dry season ends and the rains finally come, the amount of precipitation that falls in different parts of Senegal can vary greatly. In the far north, around the Senegal River, rainfall amounts average less than 20 inches (51 centimeters) each year. More precipitation occurs in the area south of the Sahel, in the Sudanian region. This part of the country usually sees between 30 to 60 inches (76 to 152 cm) of rain per year. The most rain falls in

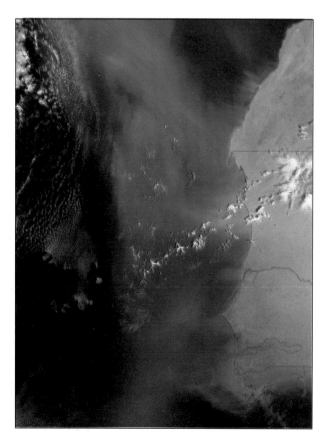

This NASA satellite image shows *harmattan* **dust storms sweeping off the west coast of Africa.**

the far southern area of Senegal known as the Casamance. It receives about 65 inches (165 cm) of precipitation each year.

However, these higher rainfall numbers do not mean the Sudanian region is immune to drought. Although the rainy season generally runs from May to November, precipitation falls mostly from July through September. During the rest of the year, the area may go for weeks without rain.

Because of the breezes that blow from off the ocean, the temperatures in Senegal's western regions are usually cooler than those in the eastern part of the country. The average temperature on the Atlantic coast hovers around 71 degrees Fahrenheit (22 degrees Celsius). Farther inland, the average temperature often climbs to around 84°F (29°C). However, there is generally less humidity inland than along the coast.

PLANTS AND ANIMALS

A land with rich biodiversity, Senegal contains approximately 2,100 plant species and nearly 1,000 animal species. In the dry Sahel to the north, various desert animals such as jackals, warthogs, and tortoises thrive. The region is also home to the dama gazelle, which feeds on desert grasses and scrubby bushes, as well as on native trees such as the acacia and baobab.

The acacia that is native to Senegal is a tree that grows to about 66 feet (20 m) high. It produces gum arabic, a natural substance used in the processing of certain foods, medicines, and cosmetics. Another tree that survives in the drought-like conditions of the Sahel is the massive baobab. It grows as high as 98 feet (30 m) tall and lives for more than a thousand years. The baobab provides African people with fruit to make drinks;

leaves to make tea and medicines; and bark to make rope, baskets, paper, mats, and cloth.

The acacia and baobab trees are also scattered throughout the *savanna* grasslands of southern Senegal. Some of the trees found in the forests of the Casamance region include the mango, coconut palm, eucalyptus, kapok, and mangrove.

Mangrove trees are common sights along the banks of the Saloum and the Casamance Rivers, as well as along the Atlantic coast. Unlike other trees, mangroves can live in salty and extremely wet conditions. They thrive in swampy areas, next to rivers, and along ocean coasts. Their stilt-like roots hold on to the soil, helping to prevent soil erosion. Mangrove tree roots also provide a breeding place for many fish and other aquatic life.

PROTECTING SENEGAL'S WILDLIFE

Like many other African countries, Senegal has seen its wildlife numbers reduced because of illegal hunting, or *poaching*, and *habitat* loss, as people clear forests and take land for agricultural use. Some species are endangered. That is, their numbers have declined so much that they are at risk of becoming extinct. In an effort to care for its plant and animal life, the Senegalese government has set aside about 11 percent of its land as reserves and protected areas.

One of the most important reserves is Niokolo-Koba National Park, which is located in eastern Senegal. The park spreads across more than 2.3 million acres (913,000 hectares), encompassing both dry savanna and forested woodland. Nearly 350 different kinds of birds and 80 different mammals, including leopards, warthogs, lions, baboons, and buffalo, live in the reserve.

Once widespread over much of the Sahara and the Sahel, the dama gazelle survives in arid regions because it obtains water from the plants that it eats. In recent years the animal's population has been severely reduced in the wild because of overhunting.

Hippopotamuses and crocodiles can be spotted in the park's rivers, marshes, and lakes.

Another significant animal sanctuary is the Djoudj National Park for Birds, located north of Saint-Louis, on Senegal's far northwestern coast. Covering more than 29,000 acres (12,000 hectares), the park is one of the world's major bird reserves. Each year its Senegal River Delta wetlands welcome nearly 3 million migrating birds. Among the more than 400 species documented annually are flamingos, pelicans, cormorants, and ducks. The park is also home to other wildlife, including jackals, hyenas, monkeys, and gazelles.

South of Saint-Louis are the National Park of the Langue de Barbarie and the Fauna Reserve of Guembuel. The reserve at the Langue de Barbarie shelters water birds such as cormorants, pink flamingos, and pelicans. Guembuel has almost 200 species of birds, as well as endangered species such as the dama gazelle, the patas monkey, and the African spurred tortoise.

Senegal's many parks and reserves play a dual role. They not only protect the native habitat and the wildlife that live there, they also bring in tourist dollars.

ENVIRONMENTAL ISSUES

In addition to poaching and habitat loss, several environmental issues are threatening Senegal. Among the most serious are deforestation (the loss of wooded areas), soil erosion and *desertification*, and overfishing.

The village of Thiokhmar, in northern Senegal, where residents have planted about 7 1/2 acres (3 hectares) of trees to stop desertification. Before the trees were planted, the Sahara Desert had been moving southward at the rate of about 43 feet (13 meters) per year.

Many people in Senegal depend on wood for fuel for cooking and for heating their homes. As the country's population has grown, more people have been cutting down trees for fuel. Trees are also being lost through logging, as some forested areas are cleared for their timber. Since 1990 the country has lost about 10 percent of its forests.

The loss of trees in the Sahel is a cause of desertification, the continuing degradation of arable land until it can no longer support any plant growth. Desertification is also caused by drought, erosion, and overgrazing. Concerned about the increasing rate of desertification in the Sahel, the government of Senegal announced in 2005 that it planned to participate with other Africa countries in the Green Wall Initiative. This program involves planting a nine-mile-wide "great green wall" of trees at the edge of the Sahara Desert, with the goal of stopping further southward desertification. The proposed "wall" would run from Senegal's capital city of Dakar to Djibouti (the capital of Djibouti, located in eastern Africa)—a distance of approximately 4,375 miles (7,000 km). So far, only about 325 miles (523 km) of that distance have been planted—all within Senegal, where national leaders has made it a priority.

With its long coastline and coastal waters rich in fish, Senegal has depended for many years on fishing to support its people and its economy. Recently, however, local fishermen have had to travel farther offshore to catch fish. They blame the depleted stock on overfishing, caused by increasing numbers of foreign fishing fleets in the country's coastal waters. Because the government of Senegal continues to grant *concessions* to foreign fishing fleets, the scarcity of fish continues to be a problem.

(Opposite) French president Jacques Chirac (left) and Senegalese president Abdoulaye Wade wave to the crowd during Chirac's 2005 visit to Africa. A former colony of France, Senegal has maintained close ties with the European country. (Right) The first president of Senegal, Léopold Sédar Senghor was respected internationally as a statesman, poet, and humanist.

2 An Ancient Past, A Promising Future

ARCHEOLOGISTS BELIEVE THAT SENEGAL has been inhabited since pre-historic times. Early people were nomads, who moved from place to place in search of the resources they needed to survive. They hunted animals and gathered fruits, nuts, and berries.

Around 800 B.C. these nomadic people began to settle into communities, establishing permanent settlements in fertile river valleys and near the ocean. Archeologists today have found tools and weapons that belonged to early peoples living along Senegal's northwestern coast, near Dakar. Another ancient society, dating as far back as the 3rd century B.C. lived in central Senegal, north of the Gambia River. This civilization left behind hundreds of "stone circles"—circular arrangements of massive stone pillars, some weighing as much as several tons.

EARLY CIVILIZATIONS

From around A.D. 300 through the 1500s, a series of West African empires controlled the eastern region of Senegal. One of the earliest was the Ghana Empire, which also included portions of today's western Mali and much of Mauritania. Founded around A.D. 750, the Ghana Empire was dominated by the Soninke, a group of Mande-speaking people who lived along the border of the southern Sahara Desert. From its Soninke capital city of Kumbi Saleh, the empire established a profitable trade of gold and salt with the Arabs from the north. By the end of the 11th century, the Ghana Empire had declined and broken up into small kingdoms that often fought among themselves.

As the Ghana Empire fell, it was replaced by the Mali Empire. Founded and initially ruled by Sundiata Keita, the Mali Empire became most powerful during the 13th and 14th centuries, when it controlled numerous gold mines and dominated trade from sub-Saharan Africa to northern and eastern

Golden artifacts created during the time of the Mali Empire are displayed alongside blocks of salt. The Mali Empire grew wealthy during the 13th and 14th centuries because of its monopoly on the trans-Saharan trade of both gold and salt.

Africa. The Mali Empire reached its peak during the 1300s, while under the rule of Mansa Musa. He used Mali's wealth to establish the city of Timbuktu (in present-day Mali) as a center of learning.

During the times of the Ghana and Mali Empires, smaller kingdoms existed in other parts of Senegal. One was the Tekrur (also spelled Tekrour) Kingdom, which controlled part of northern Senegal from the 8th to 11th centuries. During the 13th and 14th centuries, the Jolof Empire (also called the Djolof Empire) flourished in the central interior and along the western coast of Senegal. Founded by the Wolof people, the Jolof Empire eventually split apart during the 16th century. At that time, it formed several states, including the Jolof, Walo, Kajor, and Baol kingdoms.

The religious faith of Islam was introduced to Senegal through the Tekrur kingdom, whose inhabitants were converted by the Berber people living to the north. Those who follow Islam, called Muslims, follow the teachings of the Prophet Mohammad, who lived during the seventh century. In 1049 the ruler of Tekrur, War Jabi, became a Muslim. In time, most of his people converted as well. The Islamic religion eventually spread southward throughout the rest of Senegal.

BATTLING FOR CONTROL

The first Europeans to make contact with the people of Senegal were the Portuguese. In 1444 Portugal established the first of what would become many trading posts along the coast of the country. Portuguese merchants were soon trading European textiles, metal goods, and horses for African gold, ivory, and slaves.

In this engraving made in 1860, Africans endure a harsh journey across the Atlantic Ocean in a slave ship carrying them to the United States. Over the course of hundreds of years, the transatlantic slave trade, which reached its peak during the 1700s and 1800s, forced more than 20 million Africans into slavery.

The slave trade began in the 1500s, with Africans being shipped to colonies in the Americas to work on plantations. Over the years, as many as 20 million Africans would pass through slave trading centers in West Africa, on their way to forced labor in a foreign land. Portugal maintained its profitable trading network in Senegal until the late 1500s.

However, other European powers were also interested in the region. By 1600, the Portuguese had been driven out by the Dutch and French. In 1617 the Dutch West Indies Company established the first permanent European trading settlement at Goree Island, near today's city of Dakar. Goree Island would ultimately become a major slave-trading center in the region. In 1659 the French laid claim to a northern portion of Senegal's coast when they built a fort at the mouth of the Senegal River, founding the city of Saint-Louis.

Great Britain also wanted to dominate trade in the region. In the late 1600s the island of Goree fell to the English, and then to the French, who permanently ousted the Dutch settlers from the region. From the mid-1700s until the early 1800s the English and French continued to fight over the trading centers of Saint-Louis and Goree. Finally, in 1814, Great Britain and France signed the Treaty of Paris, which granted the territory of Senegal to the French and control of The Gambia to the British.

The following year, the French abolished the slave trade, although the practice of slavery remained legal in Senegal and French-controlled territories until 1848. Instead of trade in humans, agricultural trade became the focus. France established areas where workers grew *cash crops* such as cotton and groundnuts (peanuts)—crops that came originally from the Americas, not Africa. The French were also interested in profiting from the sale of a native product—gum arabic—produced by the acacia tree and used at the time in food processing and in the manufacture of ink.

A FRENCH COLONY

After making peace with Great Britain, France next looked to bringing Senegal's kingdoms under French rule. Between 1840 and 1865, French soldiers swept inland, eventually conquering the territories controlled by ethnic groups such as the Wolof, Serer, and Tukolor.

In 1895 Senegal was established as a French colony that was united with seven other French-controlled territories, including French Sudan (now known as Mali) and French Guinea (Guinea). A governor-general appointed by the French administered the new federation, which was called French West Africa. Its capital was Saint-Louis, in Senegal. In 1902, Dakar replaced Saint-Louis as the capital.

During its control over Senegal, France provided funding for economic development. To foster the transportation of West African agricultural resources to markets, the French financed the construction of a railway, completed in 1882, between Dakar and Saint-Louis. Another rail line would later be built that linked Dakar to the interior peanut-growing areas in the French Sudan and along the Niger River.

Under French colonial rule, taxes were levied on Africans, although little was done to help the *indigenous* people economically. In some areas of Senegal, however, such as Goree, Rufisque, and Saint-Louis, Africans were granted the right to elect a deputy to the French National Assembly.

THE DEMAND FOR FREEDOM

During the Second World War (1940–1945), Senegalese soldiers fought alongside troops seeking to free France from German occupation. After the war, many West Africans demanded their own freedoms—including the right to participate in their country's government.

In an effort to address the growing civil unrest, the French government passed a new constitution in 1946. It called for replacing the colonial system with a new kind of government for French-controlled lands—a federation of former colonies and territories called the French Union. French West Africa became part of this new federation, in which inhabitants of French colonies were given legal rights as citizens of France. In Senegal, African people were given the rights to run for election for seats in the French National Assembly and participate in their local governments.

An early 20th-century photograph of a village along the Senegal River. At the time this picture was taken, the French had taken control of the territory of today's Senegal, as well as lands to the north, east, and south. They were administered together as a federation called French West Africa.

The passage of yet another constitution in France in 1958 replaced the French Union with another political organization—the French Community. It included Senegal and the countries of the Central African Republic, Chad, Congo (Brazzaville), Gabon, and the Malagasy Republic. Although members of the French Community were permitted to govern themselves, they were not given control over many aspects of government. Such areas as foreign policy, defense, economic policy, the judicial system, education, currency, and communications remained under control of the French government.

INDEPENDENCE

The French Community was short-lived, breaking apart in 1959. On April 4 of that year, France officially recognized the Federation of Mali, which consisted of the independent state of Senegal united with the French Sudan. The leaders of the two former territories could not agree on how the new country should be governed. On August 20, 1960, the Mali Federation was dissolved and its member countries became independent republics. Senegal became the Republic of Senegal, and continued its ties with the French Community. The French Sudan became the Republic of Mali.

In September 1960 Léopold Sédar Senghor was elected the first president of Senegal. Educated at local missionary schools and at the University of Paris, in France, Senghor was a poet and intellectual who had served during World War II in the French army. He had been elected in 1945 to the French National Assembly, where he served until 1958. That year, he had helped found and served as secretary-general of a political party called the Senegalese Progressive Union (UPS).

Originally, the system of government in the new republic called for the sharing of power between the president and prime minister. However, two years after Senghor became president, his prime minister, Mamadou Dia, attempted to overthrow him in a coup. After the coup failed, Senghor had Dia arrested and imprisoned. Senghor then sponsored passage of a new constitution that eliminated the position of prime minister.

Because the UPS was the only legal party in the country, Senghor remained in power when subsequent elections were held, in 1968 and 1973. His rule would last 20 years.

EARLY CHALLENGES

In the late 1960s, a series of severe droughts struck in the Sahel region of northern Senegal. People throughout the country suffered from widespread food shortages. Around the same time a drop in world prices for peanuts—one of Senegal's biggest crops—also hurt the economy. The

A farmer in the drought-affected area of Senegal watering plants. 1974.

nation suffered severe economic problems, further worsened by decreases in the foreign aid normally received from France.

Economic woes led to civil unrest. In May 1968 disgruntled workers and students staged a massive demonstration that effectively paralyzed the government. In response, Senghor called out the military to help restore order. He also called on Islamic religious leaders for assistance. However, despite his efforts, civil unrest in Senegal continued throughout the early

1970s. In time, conditions improved in Senegal, and the political situation calmed.

As a result Senghor relaxed his authoritarian rule. He re-established the position of prime minister and in 1974 allowed the formation of a competing political party—the Senegalese Democratic Party (PDS). In 1978 he loosened restrictions even more, allowing for a three-party political system in the country. By that time his own party—the Senegalese Progressive Union—had been renamed the Socialist Party (PS).

In 1980 Senghor stepped down from the presidency, and Socialist Party member Abdou Diouf assumed leadership of Senegal. One of his first moves was to lift the restriction on the number of political parties allowed in Senegal.

A NEW CONFEDERATION

In 1982, in an effort to combine their military and security forces, the governments of The Gambia and Senegal formed a federation called Senegambia. However, the plan to create a strong nation by joining the military and economic forces of both countries together did not work out. In 1989 the federation was dissolved.

THE CASAMANCE CONFLICT

For many years, Senegal has been dealing with a separatist war within the country, based in the southern Casamance region. Fighting began in 1982, when the Movement for the Democratic Forces of Casamance (MFDC) started battling the Senegalese government. In late 2004 both sides signed a peace accord. However, government troops and separatists continue to clash in the region. In

In December 2004, Interior Minister Ousmane Ngom (left) signed a peace treaty to end the separatist conflict with the Movement for the Democratic Forces of Casamance (MFDC). Representing the rebel group was Father Augustin Diamacoune Senghor, a priest who had worked for years to help the region's Jola (Diola) people achieve equal rights.

December 2010, about 100 MDFC fighters attempted to capture Bignona, but were repulsed by Senegalese soldiers.

Years of conflict in Casamance have claimed hundreds of lives and displaced thousands of people. Many of them fled to safety across the border to Guinea-Bissau, where they now live in refugee camps. In Casamance buried landmines continue to pose a threat to civilians, while public buildings such as schools, hospitals, and clinics destroyed by war need to be rebuilt.

A PEACEFUL TRANSITION

In 2000 Senegal saw an end to 40 years of rule by Senegal's Socialist Party. In March of that year, Senegalese Democratic Party leader Abdoulaye Wade opposed the *incumbent* president, Diouf. Two rounds of voting were required to determine a winner. In the end, Wade garnered 58.49 percent of the vote to Diouf's 41.51 percent. In a peaceful change in government, Diouf stepped down after almost 20 years in power.

(Opposite) Senegalese president Abdoulaye Wade (left) speaks with former president Abdou Diouf at a May 2006 awards ceremony. As president, Wade oversaw efforts to end corruption and promote economic development. However, in 2012 he was defeated in his bid for a third term. (Right) A meeting of the Senegalese National Assembly, based in Dakar.

3 Democracy in Decline?

THE REPUBLIC OF SENEGAL is a multiparty democracy with a strong tradition of civilian rule. Unlike many other African nations, Senegal has experienced peaceful governmental transfers of power. In Senegal's democratic style of government, all citizens—men and women—ages 18 and older are allowed to vote in local and federal elections. Because of its relatively stable government, the country was long considered a model democracy. Recent changes, however, have called that status into question.

ADMINISTRATIVE REGIONS

For government administrative purposes, the country of Senegal is divided into 14 regions, each headed by a governor appointed by the president. Each section is named after its regional capital—Dakar, Diourbel, Fatick, Kaffrine,

Kaolack, Kédougou, Kolda, Louga, Matam, Saint-Louis, Sédhiou, Tambacounda, Thiès, and Ziguinchor. The regions of Kaffine, Kédougou, and Sédhiou were formed in 2008, when they were split off from the Kaolack, Tambacounda, and Kolda regions, respectively.

BRANCHES OF GOVERNMENT

The government is divided into three branches: executive, legislative, and judicial. The executive branch and the legislature conduct business from the capital city of Dakar.

The executive branch is led by the president, who serves as the chief of state and commander in chief of armed forces. Elected by the country's voters, the president serves a five-year term. He or she can be reelected only once. Abdoulaye Wade, who was elected president in April 2000, served a seven-year term because that length had been established under the country's previous constitution. Senegal's current constitution, which took effect in January 2001, originally limited presidential terms of office to five years. However, a year after Wade was reelected president in March 2007, the National Assembly approved a constitutional amendment that returns the presidential term to seven years after the 2012 election.

Other officials in the executive branch of government are the ministers, who oversee specific government departments such as education, environment, and industry. They are led by the prime minister, who is appointed by the president. This executive cabinet, called the Council of Ministers, consists of 37 members. The prime minister, after consulting with the president, appoints members of the Council. Some cabinet positions include the minister of foreign affairs, the minister of justice, the minister of energy and biofuels, and the minister of economy and finance.

Senegal's current constitution was approved in the spring of 2001. Several amendments since that time have served to increase executive power and reduce the power of the opposition, moving Senegal toward an increasingly autocratic style of government. A senate was instituted in 1999, abolished with the 2001 constitution, then reinstated in 2007. This changed the legislative branch of government from a *unicameral* (single chamber) system consisting of the National Assembly alone to a *bicameral* (two chamber) parliament that also includes the senate.

Idrissa Seck was Prime Minister of Senegal from November 2002 to April 2004.

The National Assembly is responsible for creating the country's laws. It consists of 150 members, called deputies, who serve five-year terms. Ninety deputies are elected by direct popular vote, while 60 are elected according to proportional representation from the various political parties. The senate consists of 100 members serving five-year terms. Thirty-five are indirectly elected by local municipal councillors, while 65 senators are appointed by the president. The next elections for Parliament are scheduled to be held in 2012.

The legal judicial system in Senegal is based on the French civil law system. It consists of lower courts, which cover civil and criminal cases, and several special higher courts. Among the high courts are the Court of Appeals, Cour de Cassation (Court of Final Appeals), and the Council of State. Also among Senegal's highest courts is the Constitutional Court, which determines the constitutionality of laws and international agreements and mediates disputes between executive and legislative branches of government. Its justices are appointed by the president.

POLITICAL PARTIES

Today more than 70 political parties exist in Senegal. Among the important groups are the Alliance of Forces for Progress (AFP), the Union for Democratic Renewal (URD), and the Independence and Labor Party (PIT).

The Socialist Party (SP) and the Senegalese Democratic Party (PDS) are two of the most powerful political parties in Senegal. They dominated the 2000 elections, in which PDS candidate Abdoulaye Wade beat SP incumbent Abdou Diouf. The elections were later hailed by the international community as an example of a peaceful, democratic transition of government, an event uncommon in Africa.

However, critics of President Wade expressed concern that his administration had tarnished Senegal's reputation for good governance. In the mid-2000s, legislative elections were rescheduled several times. When demonstrators marched in January 2007 to protest a second postponement, the Senegalese government cracked down, arresting several opposition party leaders. There was also reported civil unrest and violence linked with the presidential election campaigns.

Wade easily won reelection in the February 2007 presidential election with nearly 56 percent of the vote. His critics claimed fraud and refused to participate in the parliamentary elections held in June 2007. The low voter turnout enabled the Sopi Coalition to gain control of the National Assembly. The PDS also won 34 of the 35 directly elected seats in the Senate election, held in August 2007, and Wade appointed the remaining 65 senators.

Protests erupted across the nation when a constitutional court declared that Wade could run for a third term as president in 2012. This had originally been prohibited by the constitution. In March 2012, Wade was defeated by Macky Sall, who won 65 percent of the vote.

INTERNATIONAL ROLE

Because of its reputation for religious and ethnic tolerance, the government of Senegal has been called on to help with conflicts in other parts of the world. Some areas where Senegalese peacekeeping troops have served in recent years include the Darfur region of Sudan, Liberia, Cote d'Ivoire, Sierra Leone, Rwanda, and the Democratic Republic of the Congo.

Soldiers of the 1st Infantry Battalion Senegal army receive training on equipment and fighting tactics in preparation for their role in peace enforcement in the African country of Sierra Leone. Because of Senegal's political stability, it has frequently been called upon to provide peacekeeping forces in other parts of the world.

(Opposite) A miller pours peanuts into a grinding mill. Peanuts are a major export crop of Senegal. (Right) A Bedick weaver plies his trade. The Bedick are a minority ethnic group found in the far eastern area of Senegal.

4 A Stable Economy

SENEGAL SUFFERS FROM WIDESPREAD POVERTY, with 54 percent of its people living below the poverty line. The nation also has a high unemployment rate of around 48 percent; among its young people about 40 percent cannot find work. Despite these bleak numbers, Senegal has managed to maintain a stable economy over the years.

CONSISTENT GROWTH

Economic growth in a country is measured according to its *gross domestic product* (GDP), which is the total value of goods and services produced in year by a country's workers. workers. From 1995 through 2008, this value consistently increased in Senegal, with GDP growing an average of 5 percent per year. Many countries were affected by the 2009 downturn in the global economy. That year, the growth rate of Senegal's GDP fell to below 2 percent. However, Senegal's economy grew by nearly 4 percent in 2010, resulting in a GDP of nearly $24 billion.

Despite Senegal's stable economic growth, most of the country's wealth is concentrated in urban areas, particularly in and around Dakar. In rural parts of the country the very poor eke out a living by farming small plots of land using simple hand tools.

AGRICULTURE AND FISHING

About 708 percent of the population of Senegal makes a living by farming. However, agriculture contributes less than 15 percent to the country's GDP. For the most part, rural farmers are too poor to afford the tools that would help them increase their crop yields (such as irrigation or fertilizers). Most are subsistence farmers, who manage to raise only enough food to feed them-

Senegalese women tend to their garden in Bantantinnting, Senegal

THE ECONOMY OF SENEGAL

Gross domestic product (GDP*):
$23.88 billion

Inflation: 1.2%

Natural resources: phosphates, iron ore, gold, titanium, oil and gas

Agriculture (14.9% of GDP): peanuts, millet, corn, sorghum, rice, cotton, tomatoes, green vegetables; cattle, poultry, pigs; fish

Services (63.6% of GDP): telecommunications, tourism

Industry (21.4% of GDP): agricultural and fish processing, phosphate mining, fertilizer production, petroleum refining; iron ore, zircon, and gold mining, construction materials, ship construction and repair

Foreign trade:

Exports–$2.112 billion: fish, groundnuts (peanuts), petroleum products, phosphates, cotton

Imports–$4.474 billion: food and beverages, capital goods, fuels

Economic growth rate: 3.9%

Currency exchange rate: U.S. $1 = 507.71 *Communaute Financiere Africaine* (CFA) francs (2011)

*GDP is the total value of goods and services produced in a country annually.
All figures are 2010 estimates unless otherwise indicated.
Source: CIA World Factbook, 2011

selves and their families. Typical crops include millet (a kind of grain), cassava, tomatoes, and other vegetables.

The most important cash crop and major export in Senegal is peanuts. Most peanuts are grown on small farms around the Saloum River near the communities of Diourbel and Kaolack, in western Senegal. Other important export crops include cotton, sesame, soya, sunflowers, and rice.

In recent years, farm production in parts of Senegal has decreased because of environmental problems such as soil degradation and desertification. A series of droughts during the late 1970s and early 1980s destroyed crops and caused food shortages. Some farmers are demanding that the government provide training in better land use, funding for irrigation systems, and other support to improve agricultural productivity.

Fish serve as an important source of food in Senegal, as well as a source of export income. The government receives payments from foreign nations in exchange for allowing their fleets to fish in Senegal's coastal waters. However, overfishing has led to scarcity in fish stocks.

SERVICES

The services sector, which includes businesses such as telecommunications and tourism, makes up the majority of the Senegal's GDP—about 64 percent. Tourism and information technology are growing sectors of the economy.

Senegal's urban areas, particular Dakar, support a strong information technology sector. The capital city is located along the path of the transatlantic undersea fiber-optic cable that links Europe to Latin America. In recent years European companies looking to outsource service jobs in the call-center market have turned to Senegal for French-speaking, inexpensive labor. The result has been strong growth in jobs in the telecommunications field.

Tourism has also created thousands of jobs in Senegal, providing work in the hotel industry, catering businesses, and restaurants. According to the Senegalese National Trade Union Workers, 350,000 tourists visited Senegal in 2005. By 2008, foreign tourists to Senegal surpassed 1 million a year. The government is making plans to help tourism grow even more in the coming years. French investors are the biggest foreign investors in hotels and other tourist facilities of Senegal.

Senegalese phone-marketing operators work at the Premium Contact International Center in Dakar. The country's advanced telecommunications infrastructure has helped make the telecommunications industry one of the fastest-growing sectors of Senegal's economy.

INDUSTRY

Industry accounts for about 21 percent of Senegal's GDP, and the sector is growing. While peanut-processing ranks as a major industry, fish processing, petroleum refining, and flour milling also contribute to the country's industrial base. Other important industries include boatbuilding and the production of construction materials (including paint, cement, and limestone).

However, most income generated by industry comes from the mining of the country's natural resources. Senegal has large deposits of phosphate rock, which is mined and processed to make phosphate fertilizers and other industrial chemicals. The minerals industry also includes the mining of gold, diamonds, and iron ore. The government also has plans to develop oil reserves that have been discovered both on land and offshore.

TRANSPORTATION

Senegal has a better developed transportation system than most other African nations. More than 8,400 miles (13,576 km) of roads thread through the nation, although fewer than 2,500 miles (3,972 km) of them are paved. Railroads stretch across more than 560 miles (906 km). The country also has 20 airports, but only half of these facilities have paved runways. Efforts to improve the highways, modernize the nation's railroads, and build a new airport are among the government's top priorities.

ECONOMIC REFORMS

During the early 1990s, Senegal began to distance itself from socialist policies (in which the government owns and controls businesses) to a liberalized economy. This meant that many state-owned enterprises were privatized—sold to individuals or businesses. The goal was to reduce the role of government in the economy, and encourage the private sector to introduce better management and growth.

The Senegalese government also eliminated price controls and government *subsidies*, and it devalued the country's basic unit of currency, the CFA franc. Some economists credit these and other economic reforms with helping turn the country's economy around.

TRADE

Senegal is a member of the West African Economic and Monetary Union, an organization made up of countries that use the CFA franc as its currency.

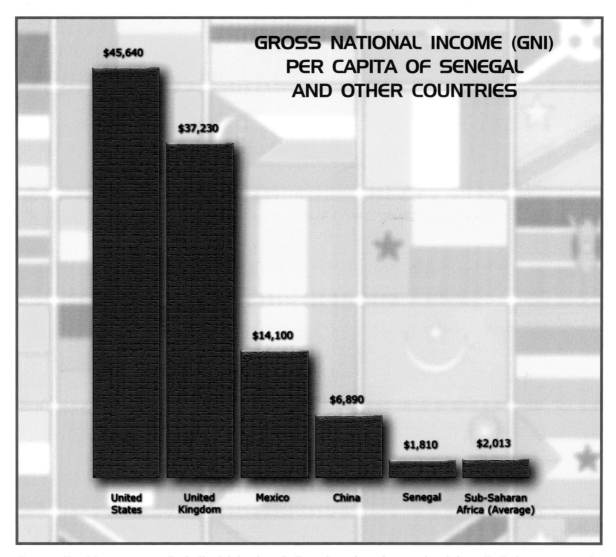

GROSS NATIONAL INCOME (GNI) PER CAPITA OF SENEGAL AND OTHER COUNTRIES

Country	GNI
United States	$45,640
United Kingdom	$37,230
Mexico	$14,100
China	$6,890
Senegal	$1,810
Sub-Saharan Africa (Average)	$2,013

Gross national income per capita is the total value of all goods and services produced domestically in a year, supplemented by income received from abroad, divided by midyear population. The above figures take into account fluctuations in currency exchange rates and differences in inflation rates across global economies, so that an international dollar has the same purchasing power as a U.S. dollar has in the United States.   Source: World Bank, 2011.

Members of the New Partnership for Africa's Development (NEPAD) meet at the Kenyatta International Conference Center in Nairobi, Kenya. Established in 2001 by African leaders, including Senegalese president Abdoulaye Wade, NEPAD attempts to address the problems of economic development in Africa.

Through this group, Senegal is working with other West African nations to establish unified *tariffs* and more stable monetary policies.

The country's leading trade partner is France. Other nations in the European Union, as well as Mali, The Gambia, India, China, Thailand, and the United States, also maintain trade with Senegal.

FOREIGN INVESTMENT AND AID

The nation's stable economic growth, along with its reputation as a stable democracy, has attracted significant foreign investment. Businesses from countries such as Japan, China, India, and the United States have financed the development of many of Senegal's industries.

Under the administration of President Wade, Senegal was one of nations that founded the New Partnership for Africa's Development (NEPAD), an initiative launched in 2001. This organization works to develop partnerships between African countries and industrialized nations. NEPAD has promised that African leaders would continue to work on economic reforms, uphold democratic principles, and strive to follow good governance policies in exchange for fair trade policies, foreign investment, and aid and debt relief from the wealthier countries.

The government of Senegal relies heavily on foreign aid. In 2010 nearly one-fourth of all government spending in Senegal was made possible by foreign assistance. The aid comes from a number of countries, including France, the United States, Canada, Japan, Germany, and Italy.

Much of this aid is distributed through the International Monetary Fund (IMF) debt relief program. The IMF is an organization of 187 countries that work together to reduce poverty, promote employment, help increase international trade, and help countries' economies grow. In 1996 the IMF established the Highly Indebted Poor Countries (HIPC) initiative to help poor nations deal with overwhelming debt. Senegal is one of several African nations to benefit from the program.

EMIGRATION

In efforts to make money, many of Senegal's impoverished inhabitants have left the country in order to find jobs in the industrialized world. The money that Senegalese emigrants living abroad send back home, called remittances, is an important source of revenue to the nation's economy. In 2007, remittances topped $900 million—about three times as much as direct investments from foreign nations. However, most of the money from remittances is used for household consumption and is not invested in local businesses.

(Opposite) The Kermel Market in Dakar offers a range of traditional handicrafts such as *suwer* (reverse-glass painting), jewelry, pottery, and hand-woven fabrics, as well as fresh fruits and vegetables. (Right) Senegalese woman in traditional dress with matching headscarves proudly pose with their children.

5 The People of Senegal

THE SENEGALESE CULTURE is a friendly one. People share a belief in *teranga*, which in Wolof (the most common native language) means "hospitality." One Senegalese proverb states: "A visitor or stranger is a king and should be treated as such."

More than 12 million people live in Senegal. Most of them belong to one of more than a dozen different ethnic groups found in the country.

MAJOR ETHNIC GROUPS

The largest ethnic group of Senegal is the Wolof people, who make up more than 40 percent of the population. They live in all regions of the country, and form the majority in the central, northern, and coastal areas around Dakar and Saint-Louis.

The second-largest indigenous group of Senegal, at about one-fourth of the population, are the Pular (also called Pulaar, Fula, or Tukulor). Most Pular people live in northern Senegal, concentrated around the Senegalese River Valley.

Another significant ethnic group in Senegal are the Serer, which comprise about 15 percent of the population. The Serer people live mostly in west-central Senegal. Smaller minority ethnic groups in Senegal include the Jola, also called Diola, who live in Casamance, and the Mandinka, who are concentrated in southeastern Senegal and in Casamance.

Although French is the country's official language, Wolof is the most widely spoken tongue. Many citizens speak other native languages, including Pular, Jola (Diola), Serer, and Mandinka.

ISLAM AND SUFISM

First introduced to the Senegal region during the 11th century, Islam quickly took root in the region. By the 19th century it was embedded in the area's political and social structure. Today, the vast majority of Senegalese—around 94 percent—are Muslims.

Senegal's Muslims follow a branch of Islam called Sufism, which is a mystical form of the religion. While Sufis believe the basic tenets of Islam, they do not follow all of the religion's orthodox practices. Sufis seek a spiritual communion with God (Allah), which they believe can be achieved through specific practices and rituals.

The Sufis of Senegal belong to one of four main religious orders, or brotherhoods—the Mouride (Muridiyya), the Tijaniyyah (whose followers are called Tijani), the Layenne, and the Qadiri (also spelled Qadiriyya or

The Mosque de Oukama in Dakar, a Muslim place of worship, is a national landmark. Although 94 percent of Senegalese are Muslims, the government recognizes both Islamic and Christian holidays.

Qadiriya). The Qadiri order is the smallest and oldest Islamic brotherhood in Senegal, while the Tijaniyyah brotherhood is the largest.

Islamic brotherhoods are headed by spiritual leaders called *marabouts*, who wield a great deal of economic and political power. Most inherit their position from their fathers. The marabouts' followers believe the leaders carry a divine grace that gives them the power to heal illness and grant salvation to others.

TRADITIONAL RELIGIONS AND CHRISTIANITY

A small percentage of the people of Senegal—about 1 percent, living mostly in Casamance or in the eastern regions of the nation—practice a traditional African religion. Many traditional African religions are based on animism. Animists believe that a spirit can be found in all natural things, including animals, stones, and trees.

Christianity came to the indigenous people of Senegal during the 19th century, as European missionaries sought to convert the native people. Because it was seen as the faith of the invading Europeans, it did not spread quickly. Today, only about 5 percent of the population is Christian—mostly Roman Catholic. The largest Christian communities are found among the Jola (Diola) people in the Casamance, the Bassari near Kedougou (in southeastern Senegal) and the Serer in the Siné-Saloum region (around the west-central coastal area).

IMPACT OF POVERTY

More than half of the people of Senegal live in poverty. In small rural villages the very poor typically live in straw- or tin-roofed huts made of mud. More than 70 percent of homes lack electricity and running water. Although many homes in major cities have electricity and indoor plumbing, the water supply does not always work. The urban poor typically live in shantytowns, in shacks that lack electrical power or plumbing.

The extreme poverty in Senegal has had a serious impact on the health of its people. Although diseases like yellow fever and malaria (which are

THE PEOPLE OF SENEGAL

Population: 12,323,252

Ethnic groups: Wolof 43.3%, Pular (also known as Fula or Tukulor) 23.8%, Serer 14.7%, Jola (Diola) 3.7%, Mandinka 3%, Soninke 1.1%, European and Lebanese 1%, other 9.4%

Age structure:
0–14 years: 42.2%
15–64 years: 54.8%
65 years and over: 3.0%

Birth rate: 32.27 births/1,000 population

Infant mortality rate: 57.7 deaths/ 1,000 live births

Death rate: 9.49 deaths/1,000 people

Population growth rate: 2.58%

Life expectancy at birth:
total population: 59.38 years
male: 57.48 years
female: 61.34 years

Total fertility rate: 4.86 children born/woman

Religions: Muslim 94%, Christian 5%, indigenous beliefs 1%

Languages: French (official), Wolof, Pulaar (also called Pular or Fula), Jola (Diola), Mandinka

Literacy: 59.1%

All figures are 2006 estimates unless otherwise indicated.
Source: CIA World Factbook, 2011; U.S. Department of State.

transmitted by mosquitoes) can be prevented by the use of insecticide-treated nets, the poor cannot afford to buy this protection. The lack of access to safe water means that thousands of people fall victim to water-borne diseases such as cholera and other diarrheal illnesses.

Like many other sub-Saharan African countries, Senegal has had to face the significant health issue of acquired immunodeficiency syndrome (AIDS) and the human immunodeficiency virus (HIV) that causes the disease. However, during the 1980s, when the disease first surfaced in Africa, the

As in many other African countries, the lack of access to potable water is a serious issue in Senegal. The problem has been resolved in this small village on the outskirts of Dakar, where local children use specially installed foot pumps to bring water from a well to the surface.

Senegalese government sponsored public information campaigns and educational programs to fight the disease. As a result Senegal has one of the lowest infection rates (1 to 2 percent) in Africa. Today, about 67,000 people in Senegal are living with HIV or AIDS. About 1,800 Senegalese die each year from the disease.

Education in Senegal has also suffered because of the country's poverty. Less than 60 percent of Senegalese above the age of 15 are *literate*, or can read and write. Although Senegalese law requires that children attend school for at least six years, the law is not enforced. About 55 percent of Senegalese children go to elementary school, but only about 10 percent continue on to high school. Even fewer attend college.

In an effort to increase literacy, the Senegalese government now allocates around 40 percent of its budget to education. The money is being used to build new facilities in rural areas, repair and refurbish existing schools, and provide more training for teachers and school administrators.

School facilities are simple in impoverished rural parts of Senegal, such as this Bedick village near Kedougou, in the far southeastern corner of the country.

DRESS

Many Senegalese men living in urban areas have adopted European-style fashions, by wearing suits and ties. Young people in more modern cities, like Dakar, often sport jeans and t-shirts.

The traditional dress is the **boubou**, an ankle-length, flowing gown. Muslim men often wear *grand boubous* with baggy pants, and an embroidered shirt underneath. Women may dress in brightly colored *boubous* with matching skirts and blouses. Senegalese women sometimes complement their dress by adding matching scarves twisted into intricate patterns in their hair.

FOOD

The basic staple food in Senegal is millet or rice. Many people consider *ceeb u jen* (also spelled *tiéboudienne*)—a vegetable, rice, and fish dish seasoned with herbs and spices—to be Senegal's national dish. Other meals typically include meats such as goat, sheep, or chicken, which are also served with rice and vegetables.

At mealtimes in Senegal, everyone gathers around a large table or in a circle, while sitting on woven mat on the floor. Food is served in a large bowl placed in the center of the circle. After most meals, the Senegalese often enjoy a cup of tea. Local juices include *bissap* (made from hibiscus) and *bouyi* (made from the fruits of the baobab).

SPORTS

Among the most popular sports in Senegal are soccer and basketball, played on city streets and public beaches. Basketball is one of the fastest-growing sports in Africa. Organized basketball clubs exist for boys and girls in some of Senegal's major cities, and many schools sponsor teams. Senegal also has national soccer and basketball teams that have participated in competitions around the world.

Some people may argue that wrestling is truly Senegal's national sport. It is called *laamb* by the Wolof, who practice it using ancient rites and rituals. The sporting event is actually an elaborate ceremony. Drummers and singers perform before the actual match as the wrestler, wearing amulets or other charms to protect against evil spirits, dances around the arena. In Senegal, national champions are celebrated, and posters and billboards displaying wrestling heroes are commonly seen in marketplaces and along thoroughfares.

DeSagana Diop is one of several Senegalese basketball players who have reached the NBA.

MUSIC AND DANCE

Music and dance are an essential part of many life events, such as births, baby-naming ceremonies, and weddings. But music, particularly drumming, plays an important part in many other kinds of gatherings, including sports events and religious or political meetings.

In Senegal, traditional music and dance is commonly accompanied by the *sabar*, a Wolof drum that is made in various shapes and sizes. Different tones from groups of different sabars create the necessary sound and rhythm. Traditional sabar dance rhythms are also found in contemporary Senegalese music known as *mbalax*. During the 1980s musician Youssou N'Dour achieved international fame by blending traditional Senegalese music with

A merchant offers a variety of hand-carved items for sale at a dockside display. Artisans typically create carvings from ebony and other hardwoods, using simple hand tools.

modern sounds. Baaba Maai is another Senegalese singer who has become popular around the world.

Another important drum in West Africa is the *tama*, or "talking drum." This is a small drum held under the arm and squeezed to tighten the drum head, thus changing the pitch. These variations in pitch can mimic language, which gives the talking drum its name. Tamas are often used to accompany dancing or chanting by **griots**, or storytellers. Tamas are also used in Senegalese contemporary pop music.

ARTWORK AND LITERATURE

A unique style of Senegalese artwork is **suwer**, or reverse-glass painting. The name comes from the French expression "sous-verre," meaning "under the glass." After being painted, the glass is fired, which makes the image permanent. Suwer has been practiced since the early 1900s in Senegal.

Senegal's artisans create many other forms of handicraft, including pottery, baskets, jewelry, and bright-colored fabrics. Wood-carvers fashion detailed figures from ebony wood, while sand painters create images using colored sand from various parts of the country.

The arts and culture of Africa were of great interest to Senegal's first president, Léopold Senghor, who was himself a renowned poet. During the 1930s, while living in Paris, Léopold Sédar Senghor helped develop a concept called *négritude*. This literary movement called for the restoration of the African cultural identity and protested against French colonial rule. In his poetry Senghor described the hardships black Africans were enduring in Senegal; his first works were published in 1945.

(Opposite) The cosmopolitan urban center of Dakar is a major regional port, as well as the site of an international airport and major railroad line terminus. (Right) Goree Island served from the 1500s to the 1800s as a holding center for African slaves being sent to the Americas. Today, the island's infamous House of Slaves is a museum.

6 Blending Past and Present

THE BOOMING TOURIST INDUSTRY along the coast of Senegal has helped modernize its larger cities. Some urban areas offer cybercafes and gleaming high rises. But within these cities it is often possible to find buildings that date back for hundreds of years, to Senegal's French colonial past.

DAKAR

With a population of nearly 2.8 million, Dakar is Senegal's largest city and an administrative and economic center. The cosmopolitan capital is nestled near the center of Senegal's Atlantic coast, on a *peninsula* called Cape Verde. This section of the continent juts farther to the west than any other part of mainland Africa.

Dakar was founded in 1857 by the French, when they built a fort on the site of a fishing village. It has been a capital city of various political entities: French West Africa, beginning in 1902; the Mali Federation, in 1959; and the Republic of Senegal, in 1960. Today, Dakar is Senegal's most important seaport: three-fourths of all the nation's foreign trade passes through the city. It is also a major transportation hub, served by an international airport—Dakar-Yoff-Léopold Sédar Senghor International Airport—which is a main stopping point for flights traveling from Europe to South America. The city's vital industrial center features factories that produce cement, soap, shoes, and textiles. Additional major industries include food processing and printing.

Visitors to Dakar can browse marketplaces, such as the Kermel and the Sandaga, that offer a variety of goods, ranging from fresh fruits and vegetables, spices, and fish to flowers, jewelry, fabric, and crafts. A popular tourist site is the Théodore Monod African Art Museum, also known as the Institut Fondamental d'Afrique Noire (IFAN). Created in 1936 by the French colonial government, this museum houses a collection of West African art and artifacts, including masks, statues, musical instruments, traditional dress, and agricultural tools. A landmark in the city is the Palais Présidentiel, the presidential palace built in 1906. Dakar also has the country's largest university—Cheikh Anta Diop University, also known as the University of Dakar. It is named for one of Senegal's most famed historians and archeologists.

TOUBA

One of Senegal's fastest growing cities is Touba, which had a population in 1958 of just 2,000, and today is home to more than 500,000. Located in west-central Senegal, the holy city is the base of the Mouride Sufi brotherhood, a large and influential Islamic sect founded by the *marabout* Amadou Bamba (1850–1927). He established the city of Touba in 1887.

The Mouride brotherhood celebrates a religious festival 48 days after the Islamic New Year. Called the Grand Magal, the pilgrimage and holiday commemorate the return from exile of Bamba, who had been forced out of Senegal by the French. Each year 1 to 2 million Mourides travel to Touba to pray at the Grand Mosque, which contains the spiritual leader's tomb.

THIÈS

Located in west-central Senegal, Thiès is the country's third-largest city, with a population of around 320,000. The city sits at the juncture of two major rail lines and is an important railroad transportation center, a major livestock-trading market, and a meatpacking center. Another important industry is mineral processing—substantial phosphate deposits that are mined in the surrounding region are processed at Thiès. The city is also famous for its tapestry factory, the Manufactures Sénégalaises des Arts Décoratifs, which produces textiles based on paintings by Sengalese artists.

MBOUR

An important harbor town, Mbour is located about 50 miles (80 km) south of Dakar. With a population of more than 180,000, Mbour is Senegal's fourth-largest city. Among the city's major industries are fishing, peanut processing, and the processing of titanium ore, which is mined nearby.

KAOLACK

Often referred to as Senegal's "peanut basin," Kaolack is a regional capital and trading center not only for peanuts (farmers bring them to the city to be cleaned and stored before being transported to factories for processing) but also for gold, cloth, and electrical equipment. Located in western Senegal, this important river port has a population of about 180,000. Among Kaolack's tourist attractions are a Moroccan-style mosque and the second-largest covered market in Africa.

SAINT-LOUIS

Founded in 1659 at the mouth of the Senegal River, in northwest Senegal, Saint-Louis was the first French settlement in Africa. The town quickly grew into a dynamic port and important commercial center. Today, Saint-Louis is the nation's second-largest seaport, with peanuts, hides, and skins serving as some of its major exports.

Today, more than 176,000 people live in the city, which is an important administrative center, fishing community, and tourist destination. Saint-Louis boasts museums, a dance company, and many other cultural opportunities, including an international jazz festival held each spring. In recent decades Saint-Louis has seen strong growth in its tourist industry, as visitors come to admire the colonial charm of the city's many 18th-and 19th-century buildings. In 2000 United Nations Educational, Scientific, and Cultural Organization (UNESCO) classified Saint-Louis as a World Heritage site.

Founded in 1659, Saint-Louis was the first French settlement in Africa. Many of the structures built in the city during the 17th and 18th centuries, such as the one shown here, have been restored.

One of the most beautiful parts of the city is the Faidherbe Bridge, which crosses the Senegal River, and links the Island of Saint-Louis with the mainland. Originally built to cross the Danube River in Europe, the bridge was shipped to the city in 1897. The structure was named for Commander Louis Faidherbe, a former governor of French Senegal.

GOREE ISLAND

Located in the harbor of Dakar, Goree Island served as a slave-trading post for hundreds of years. The first Portuguese slave house was built there in 1536. Later, the French continued to use Goree Island as a base from which African slaves were sent to the Caribbean and Louisiana. Today, many tourists come to see the House of Slaves, which now serves as a museum. In 1978, because of the island's role in the transatlantic slave trade, UNESCO designated Goree Island as a World Heritage Site.

Influences of the various European countries that occupied Goree throughout its history can be seen in the architecture. Many historical buildings can be found on the island, including the oldest mosque in the country.

A CALENDAR OF SENEGALESE FESTIVALS

January

January marks the celebration of **New Year's Day**, on January 1.

February

Confederation Day is celebrated on February 1. It commemorates the day Senegal and The Gambia formed Senegambia.

April

On April 4 people celebrate **Independence Day**, which falls on the date in 1960 that the Senegal became independent from France.

May

May 1 is **Labor Day**, which is also celebrated in many other countries to recognize the contributions of workers to their national economy.

August

August 15 is a Christian holiday called **Assumption Day**. It marks the day Mary, the mother of Jesus Christ, was taken to heaven.

November

The Christian holiday known as the **Feast of All Saints' Day** falls on November 1. The day honors all saints in the Roman Catholic and Anglican Church.

December

On December 25, Christians celebrate **Christmas Day**. This day honors the birth of Jesus Christ. During the weeks around Christmas, the residents of Saint-Louis host **Les Fanals**, or the festival of decorated lanterns.

Religious Observances

Senegal's Muslims and Christians observe the holy days of their religions. Some of these fall on specific days of each year; for example, **Christmas** (which celebrates the birth of Jesus Christ) is always observed on December 25. Many other major celebrations occur according to the lunar calendar, in which the months correspond to the phases of the moon. A lunar month is shorter than a typical month of the Western calendar. As a result, the dates of these holidays will vary from year to year.

A very important month of the Muslim lunar calendar is the ninth month, **Ramadan**. This is a time of sacrifice for devout Muslims. During Ramadan, Muslims are not supposed to eat or drink between sunup and sundown. They are also supposed to restrict their activities during these hours to necessary duties, such as going to work. After the sun has set completely, Muslims make a special prayer before eating a small meal. Muslims mark the end of Ramadan in Senegal with a celebration called **Korite** (also known as **Eid al-Fitr**, or "the breaking of the fast"). During this time families get together and exchange gifts.

Tabaski, or **Eid al-Adha** (the Feast of the Sacrifice) takes place in the last month of the Muslim calendar during the *hajj* period, when Muslims make a pilgrimage to Mecca. The holiday honors the prophet Abraham, who was willing to sacrifice his own son to Allah (God). In the story, God provided a sheep to be sacrificed instead. According to tradition, Muslim families slaughter and eat a sheep on this day. On Eid al-Adha, families traditionally eat a portion of the feast and donate the rest to the poor.

Another holy day in Senegal is **Maouloud**, or **Mawlid al-Nabiy** (the Birth of the Prophet). Muslims celebrate this day with prayer and often a procession to the local mosque. Families gather for feasts, which often feature the foods said to have been favored by Mohammed: dates, grapes, almonds, and honey. The holiday falls on the 12th day of the third month of the Islamic calendar, known as Rabi'-ul-Awwal.

Muslims in Senegal celebrate **Tamkharit**, the Islamic New Year. While not considered a major holiday by Sufis, the day is celebrated by many Senegalese by exchanging cards. In some areas children walk from house to house, singing songs.

The major Christian festivals that fall according to the lunar calendar involve the suffering and death of Jesus Christ. **Ash Wednesday** marks the start of a period of self-sacrifice called **Lent**, which lasts for 40 days. The final days of Lent are known as **Holy Week**. During this time a number of important days are observed, including **Palm Sunday**, which commemorates Jesus' arrival in Jerusalem; **Holy Thursday**, which marks the night of the last Supper; **Good Friday**, the day of Jesus' death on the cross; and **Easter Monday**, which marks his resurrection. (In Western countries, Easter is typically celebrated on the day before.)

Christians in Senegal celebrate **Pentecost,** which falls on the seventh Sunday after Easter. On that day, which celebrates the gift of the Holy Spirit to the disciples of Jesus, Christians make a pilgrimage to the coastal village of Popenguine, south of Dakar. There they pay homage to the statue of the Virgin Mary, *Notre Dame de Popenguine*, in the local church. The Christian holiday commemorating Christ's ascension into heaven after his resurrection is **Ascension Day**, which is celebrated 40 days after Easter Sunday.

The national holidays of Senegal include many Muslim and Christian holy days. The government observes the Islamic holy days of Tabaski, Tamkharit, the Birth of the Prophet, and Korite. Christian holy days that are national holidays include Easter Monday, Ascension, Pentecost, Feast of the Assumption, All Saint's Day, and Christmas.

Other Festivals

Several other festivals and special events take place throughout the year in Senegal. July 14, for example, is **African Community Day**, or Day of Association. It is dedicated to promoting the goals of African culture. August 23 celebrates the Tirailleur Senegalaise, Senegalese soldiers who fought on behalf of the French from 1857 through the early 20th century, including extensive service in World War I. Major art, music, and sports events are also held at various times throughout the year.

RECIPES

Senegal Stew

(Serves 4)
2 medium onions
2 garlic cloves
17.5 oz. cabbage
2 Tbsp. cooking oil
10.5 oz. cauliflower
9 oz. carrots
16 oz. sweet potatoes
7 oz. dried chickpeas
16 oz. millet
14 oz. can tomatoes
1 cup vegetable stock
2 Tbsp. peanut butter
1/2 tsp. ground red pepper
1/2 tsp. ground ginger
1/2 tsp. cumin
1/2 tsp. ground coriander
1/2 tsp. thyme

Directions:
1. Soak the chickpeas overnight and prepare as described on the package.
2. Slice the vegetables into chunks. In a large pan, heat the oil and stir fry the cabbage, garlic, and onions until softened, about three or four minutes.
3. Add the herbs and spices and then stir in the rest of the vegetables, including the chickpeas.
4. Bring to a boil, and then turn down and simmer with the cover on for 30 minutes.
5. Cook the millet in one liter of boiling water for about 20 minutes. Serve the millet in a separate dish.

Banana Ice Cream

(Serves 8)
8 ripe bananas
1 pint heavy cream
1/2 cup sugar

Directions:
1. In a blender, beat 4 of the bananas to a pulp. Add the heavy cream and sugar, then blend until frothy.
2. Pour the banana mixture into an 8 x 8 baking dish. Cover and place in freezer for 1-2 hours until partially firm.
3. Cut the remaining 4 bananas into quarters by slicing them down the length first, then across the middle. There should be 16 pieces.
4. Place two pieces of banana on each plate. Spread the frozen bananas over the banana slices. Sprinkle with raisins, peanuts, almonds, chocolate sauce, or colored sprinkles. Yum!

Cinq Centimes (Five-Cent Cookies)

(Serves 12)
12 3-inch sugar cookies
12 Tbsp. peanut butter
12 tsp. coarsely chopped peanuts

Directions:
1. Spread 1 tablespoon of peanut butter on top of each cookie.
2. Sprinkle each cookie with a teaspoon of chopped peanuts.

Salad with Chopped Eggs

(Serves 8)
2 cups lettuce
1 cup spinach
4 hard-boiled eggs

Directions:

1. Cut the lettuce and spinach into coarse chunks and place in eight individual salad bowls.
2. Chop up the eggs and sprinkle pieces in mounds on top of the greens.
3. Serve with dressing for salad with chopped eggs.

Dressing for Salad with Chopped Eggs

(Serves 8)
1 cup salad oil
1/2 cup tarragon vinegar
1 tsp. garlic powder
1 tsp. ground pepper
1 Tbsp. salad herbs
2 Tbsp. honey

Directions:

1. Combine all the ingredients in a jar. Tightly secure the jar with a lid and shake well.
2. Serve separately with the salad with chopped eggs.

Ceeb u jen (*Tiéboudienne*)

(Serves 8)

1 cup onions, finely chopped
1/2 cup green peppers, chopped
1 tsp. salt
1/4 tsp. cayenne pepper
4 oz. oil or margarine
6-oz. can tomato paste
2 1/4 cups water
4 lb. fish fillet (haddock or halibut)
1 head of cabbage
4 sweet potatoes
1 4 oz. jar whole pimientos
8 cups cooked rice

Directions:

1. In a 6-quart Dutch oven, sauté the onions and green peppers in the oil or margarine. Add salt and cayenne pepper. After the vegetables are lightly browned, add tomato paste and water and stir until well blended.
2. Cut fish into 8 1/2-lb. pieces and place at bottom of pan. Cut cabbage into 2-inch wide wedges. Place one wedge on top of each portion of fish.
3. Cut sweet potatoes in half and place each half on top of cabbage wedges. Cover tightly and simmer over low heat for one hour, or until vegetables and fish are done.
4. Add jar of pimientos and cook for another 2 minutes. Serve each of the eight individual portions over one cup of cooked rice.

69

GLOSSARY

bicameral—having one chamber or house.

boubou—ankle-length, flowing African garment.

Casamance—southern region of Senegal, located south of the Gambia River.

cash crops—plants grown primarily for sale on the market.

concession—legal right to manage or use the resources of an area or region for profit.

desertification—process in which land degrades so much it cannot support plant life.

estuary—area where freshwaters of a river meet the salt water of the ocean.

griot—a West African storyteller.

gross domestic product—the total value of goods and services produced in year by a country's workers.

habitat—the environment in which a plant or animal normally lives.

harmattan—a strong, damaging wind that blows off the Sahara into West Africa.

incumbent—someone who currently holds a political office.

indigenous—native to; having originated in a particular area.

literate—able to read and write.

marabout—the leader of a Sufi brotherhood, which is a religious order of Islam.

mbalax—contemporary popular music from The Gambia and Senegal that includes traditional *sabar* drum rhythms.

peninsula—a portion of land almost completely surrounded by water but connected to a larger land mass.

poaching—the practice of killing animals illegally.

rainforest—wooded area with 100 inches (254 cm) or more of rainfall per year.

sabar—a traditional drum of the Wolof people.

Sahel—a wide band of semi-arid land that lies in northern Africa, just south of the Sahara Desert.

savanna—grassland plains.

suwer—an art form traditional to Senegal in which portraits or scenes are painted on glass.

subsidy—money granted by the government to a private person or company.

tama—traditional "talking drum" of Western Africa; the variations in pitch produced by squeezing the drum can mimic human speech.

tariffs—taxes or charges placed on imported goods.

unicameral—having one chamber or house.

PROJECT AND REPORT IDEAS

Symbolism of the Flag

Research information about Senegal's national flag. Draw and color a picture of it. To complement your artwork, write a report about the history of the flag and what its colors and symbols represent.

Baobab Tree Timeline

Find a large sheet of unlined paper. On the left half of the paper, draw a picture of a baobab tree. Make sure the tree stretches the entire height of the paper. To the right of your artwork, draw 10 horizontal lines out from the right of the tree. Make sure the lines divide the paper in 10 equal sections. Each section will represent 100 years of the tree's life. The top section represents the last 100 years, the section below it represents the century before that, and so on. The bottom section of the tree represents 1,000 years ago, or when the tree was just beginning to grow. In each section, detail some historic event that occurred during that era. You can list events that happened just in Africa or that happened throughout the world as your baobab tree was "growing."

Go on a Safari

Research and write a report on one of the many animals that make their home in Senegal. Be sure to include the animal's regular habitat, what it eats, other animals that prey on it, and whether it is an endangered species. Draw a picture or make a model of the animal to go with your report.

PROJECT AND REPORT IDEAS

Research Report

Chose one of Senegal's major ethnic groups and prepare a report or poster on its traditions, history, and culture. Include a map of Senegal in your report that shows where most members of this ethnic group live.

Biography

Chose a name from the following list of people who were or are from Senegal. Research information about this person and write a one-page biography about him or her:

- Mariama Ba
- Amadou Bamba
- Madior Boye
- Abdou Diouf
- Cheikh Anta Diop
- Baaba Maal
- Youssou N'Dour
- Ousmane Sembene
- Léopold Sédar Senghor
- Abdoulaye Wade

CHRONOLOGY

800 B.C.:   Nomadic tribes begin forming more permanent settlements in the area that is now known as Senegal.

A.D. 300:   A series of West African empires emerge in the region.

700:   Ghana Empire includes part of present-day Senegal.

1100s–1300s: Jolof Empire comes into power.

1400s: Portuguese sailors begin exploring the Casamance, Senegal, and Gambia Rivers and begin trading with people living inland.

late 1500s: English, French, and Dutch traders push the Portuguese out of Senegal.

1617:   The first European trading settlement is established by the Dutch West Indies Company at Goree Island.

1659:   The French found Saint-Louis at the mouth of the Senegal River.

1677:   The Dutch are ousted from Goree Island by the French.

1814:   The Treaty of Paris cedes most of what is now Senegal to France.

1895:   Senegal becomes part of French West Africa; Saint-Louis is designated as the capital.

1902:   Dakar replaces Saint-Louis as capital of French West Africa.

1946:   Senegal becomes part of the French Union.

1958:   The country becomes a republic that is part of the French Community.

1960:   In April, Senegal gains its independence from France as part of the Mali Federation; in August, the country becomes a separate republic. Léopold Sédar Senghor is elected president.

1962:   Attempted coup by prime minister Mamadou Dia fails; Senghor strengthens the powers of the presidency.

1966:   Senegalese Progressive Union becomes only legal political party.

1970:   Senghor appoints Abdou Diouf as prime minister.

1974:   Senghor begins loosening restrictions against parties that oppose his party.

1978:   Three-party political system introduced; Goree Island is designated a World Heritage Site by UNESCO.

1980:   Senghor retires as president and is replaced by Diouf.

1982:   Senegal joins with The Gambia to form Senegambia; fighting erupts in the Casamance region between the government and a rebel group called the Movement of Democratic Forces of Casamance.

1989:   The union between Senegal and The Gambia is dissolved.

2000:   Senegalese Democratic Party leader Abdoulaye Wade defeats Diouf and becomes the first person outside the Socialist Party to be elected president of Senegal.

2001:   Senegal's government adopts a new constitution.

2002:   First woman prime minister of Senegal, Madior Boye, is appointed.

2004:   Government forces and rebels from the Movement of Democratic Forces of Casamance sign a peace agreement.

2006:   New fighting breaks out between government and rebels of the Casamance Movement of Democratic Forces.

2007:   Incumbent president Abdoulaye Wade is re-elected.

2008:   Kaffine, Kédougou, and Sedhiou regions formed, creating a total of 14.

2009:   A new gold mine, at Sabodala, begins production in March; Soulayemane Ndene Ndiaye appointed as prime minister.

2010:   The growth rate of Senegal's gross domestic product (GDP) rebounds to 4 percent after the worldwide economic downturns of 2008-2009.

2011:   New Partnership for Africa's Development (NEPAD), which develops partnerships between African countries and industrialized nations, celebrates its 10-year anniversary.

2012:   In March, Macky Sall is elected president; he takes office on April 2.

FURTHER READING/INTERNET RESOURCES

Gritzner, Janet H. *Senegal*. Philadelphia: Chelsea House, 2004.

Mason, Antony. *People Around the World*. New York: Kingfisher, 2002.

Ross, Eric S. *Culture and Customs of Senegal*. Westport, Conn.: Greenwood Press, 2008

Streissguth, Thomas. *Senegal in Pictures*. Minneapolis, Minn.: Twenty-First Century Books, 2009.

Weintraub, Aileen. *Discovering Africa's Land, People, and Wildlife (Continents of the World)*. Berkeley Heights, N.J.: Myreportlinks.com Books, 2004.

Travel Information

http://travel.state.gov/travel/cis_pa_tw/cis/cis_1013.html
http://www.lonelyplanet.com/senegal
http://www.world66.com/africa/senegal

History and Geography

http://news.bbc.co.uk/2/hi/africa/country_profiles/1064496.stm
http://www.state.gov/r/pa/ei/bgn/2862.htm

Economic and Political Information

https://www.cia.gov/library/publications/the-world-factbook/geos/sg.html
http://www.countryfacts.com/senegal/economy/

Culture and Festivals

http://www.senegal-tourism.com
http://www.worldtravelguide.net/data/sen/sen.asp
http://whats4eats.com/4rec_seneg.html

Embassy of the Republic of Senegal
2112 Wyoming Avenue NW
Washington, DC 20008
Tel: (202) 234-0540
Fax: (202) 332-6315
Website: http://www.ambasenegal-us.org

Embassy of the United States of America
American Embassy Dakar
BP 49
Avenue Jean XXIII, angle Rue Kleber
Dakar, Senegal
Tel: (221) 829-2100
Fax: (221) 822-2991
Website: http://dakar.usembassy.gov/

Senegal Tourist Office
The Pinnacle Building
3455 Peachtree Road NE
Atlanta, GA 30326
Tel: (404) 995-6628
Email: sentouroffice@aol.com
Website: http://www.senegal-tourism.com

INDEX

administrative regions, 33–34
    See also government
African religion (traditional), 52
    See also religion
agriculture, 40, 41
    See also economy
AIDS, 53–54
Alliance of Forces for Progress
    (AFP), 35
area, 11, 13
artwork, 59

borders, 11–12, 13

Casamance, 12, 30–31
Casamance River, 12–13
Christianity, 52
    See also religion
cities
    Dakar, 25, 61–62
    Goree Island, 24–25, *61*, 65
    Kaolack, 64
    Mbour, 63
    Saint-Louis, 25, 64–65
    Thiès, 63
    Touba, 62–63
climate, 13–15
constitution, 34, 35
    See also government
Constitutional Court, 35
Corniche District Mosque, *51*
Council of Ministers, 34
    See also government
Council of State, 35
    See also government
Court of Appeals, 35
Court of Final Appeals, 35

Dakar, 25, 61–62
desertification, 18–19, 40
Dia, Mamadou, 28
Diouf, Abdou, 30, 31, *33*, 35
Djoudj National Park for Birds, 17
dress, 56
droughts, 28–29
Dutch West Indies Company, 24
    See also history

economy, 28–29, 39–40, 44–47
    agriculture, 40, 41
    fishing, 40–41
    industry, 41, 43
    services, 41–43
education, 54–55
environmental problems, 18–19, 40
ethnic groups, 25, 49–50, 53

Faidherbe, Louis, 65
Faidherbe Bridge, 65
Fauna Reserve of Guembuel, 17–18
fishing, 40–41
food, 56
foreign investment, 46–47
    See also economy
France, 24–27, 44
French Community, 27–28
    See also history
French West Africa, 25–27, 62
    See also history

The Gambia, 30, 31
Gambia River, 12–13
geographic features, 11–15
Ghana Empire, 22
    See also history

Goree Island, 24–25, *61*, 65
government, 28, 31, 33–37
Grand Magal, 63
Great Britain, 24–25
Green Wall Initiative, 19
gross domestic product (GDP), 39, 41
    See also economy
gross national income (GNI), 45, 47
    See also economy

health care, 52–54
history
    Casamance conflict, 30–31
    civil unrest, 29–30
    early civilizations, 21–23
    European exploration, 23–25
    as French colony, 25–27
    independence, 27–29
    slave trade, 24–25
House of Slaves museum, *61*, 65

independence, 27–29
Independence and Labor Party
    (PIT), 35
industry, 41, 43
    See also economy
infrastructure, 26, 43–44
International Monetary Fund (IMF),
    47
Islam, 23, 50–51
    See also religion

Jola people, 50
Jolof Empire, 23
    See also history
judicial system, 35
    See also government

Numbers in **bold italic** refer to captions.

INDEX

Kaolack, 64
Kermel Market, *49*, 62
Kumbi Saleh (city), 22

laamb (wrestling), 57
languages, 50, 53
literacy rate, 53, 54–55
literature, 59

Maal, Baaba, 57
Mali Empire, 22–23
    See also history
Mali Federation, 27–28
    See also history
Mandinka people, 50
Mansa Musa, 23
Mbour, 63
Mohammad, 23
    See also Islam
Movement for the Democratic
    Forces of Casamance (MFDC),
    30–31
music and dance, 57–58

National Assembly, 34–36
    See also government
National Park of the Langue de
    Barbarie, 17
N'Dour, Youssou, 57
Népen Diakha, 12
New Partnership for Africa's
    Development (NEPAD), 46
Ngom, Ousmane, *31*
Niokolo-Koba National Park, 16–17

plants, 15–16
political parties, 28, 30, 35

See also government
population, 49, 53
Portugal, 23–24
poverty, 39, 52–54
    See also economy
Pular people, 50

religion, 50–52, 53

Sahel, 14–15
Saint-Louis, 25, 64–65
Sall, Macky, 37
Saloum River, 12
Senegal
    area, 11, 13
    borders, 11–12, 13
    cities, 61–65
    climate, 13–15
    culture, 56–59
    economy, 28–29, 39–47
    education, 54–55
    environmental problems, 18–19
    ethnic groups, 25, 49–50, 53
    geographic features, 11–15
    government, 28, 31, 33–37
    history, 21–31
    independence, 27–29
    population, 49, 53
    religion, 50–52, 53
    wildlife and plants, 15–18
Senegal River, 12
Senegalese Democratic Party (PDS),
    30, 35–37
Senegalese Progressive Union (UPS),
    28
Senegambia, 30
Senghor, Augustin Diamacoune, *31*

Senghor, Léopold Sédar, *21*, 28–30, 59
Serer people, 25, 50
services, 41–43
    See also economy
slave trade, 24–25
Socialist Party (PS), 30, 31, 35
sports, 56
Sufism, 50–51
    See also religion
Sundiata Keita, 22

Tekrur Kingdom, 23
    See also history
Thiès, 63
Touba, 62–63
tourism, 41, 43
    See also economy
Treaty of Paris, 25
    See also history

Union for Democratic Renewal
    (URD), 35

Wade, Abdoulaye, 19, *21*, 31, *33*, 34,
    35, 37
War Jabi, 23
West African Economic and
    Monetary Union, 44
wildlife, 15, 16–18
Wolof people, 23, 25, 49
World War II, 26

CONTRIBUTORS/PICTURE CREDITS

Professor Robert I. Rotberg is Director of the Program on Intrastate Conflict and Conflict Resolution at the Kennedy School, Harvard University, and President of the World Peace Foundation. He is the author of a number of books and articles on Africa, including *A Political History of Tropical Africa* and *Ending Autocracy, Enabling Democracy: The Tribulations of Southern Africa.*

Tanya Mulroy earned a bachelor's degree in special education from Moorhead State University in Moorhead, Minnesota. She worked as a special education teacher in Massachusetts. She now spends her days writing and spending time with her family at their home in Boston, Massachusetts.